P9-BYW-656

OFFICIALLY
WITHDRAWN

Jul 2015

COLONIAL AMERICA

Enzo George

Cavendish Square
New York

Palatine Public Library District
700 N. North Court
Palatine, IL 60067-8159

Published in 2015 by Cavendish Square Publishing, LLC
243 5th Avenue, Suite 136, New York, NY 10016

© 2015 Brown Bear Books Ltd

First edition

Website: cavendishsq.com

This publication represents the opinions and views of the author based on his or her personal experiences, knowledge, and research. The information in this book serves as a general guide only. The author and publisher have used their best efforts in preparing this book and disclaim liability rising directly or indirectly from the use and application of this book.

CPSIA compliance information: Batch #WW15CSQ.

All websites were available and accurate when this book was sent to press.

Library of Congress Cataloging-in-Publication Data

George, Enzo.
 Colonial America / Enzo George.
    pages cm. — (Primary sources in US history)
 Includes index.
 ISBN 978-1-50260-256-5 (hardcover) ISBN 978-1-50260-253-4 (ebook)
 1. United States—History—Colonial period, ca. 1600-1775—Sources—Juvenile literature. I. Title.

 E188.G37 2015
 973.2—dc23

                          2014024977

For Brown Bear Books Ltd:
Editorial Director: Lindsey Lowe
Managing Editor: Tim Cooke
Children's Publisher: Anne O'Daly
Design Manager: Keith Davis
Designer: Lynne Lennon
Picture Manager: Sophie Mortimer

Picture Credits:
T=Top, C=Center, B=Bottom, L=Left, R=Right

Front Cover : FC All images Library of Congress
All images © Library of Congress, except; 10, © Bettmann/Corbis; 30, © Shutterstock.

Brown Bear Books has made every attempt to contact the copyright holder.
If you have any information please contact licensing@brownbearbooks.co.uk.

We believe the extracts included in this book to be material in the public domain.
Anyone having any further information should contact licensing@brownbearbooks.co.uk.

All rights reserved. No part of this book may be reproduced, stored in a retrieval system, or transmitted in any form or by any means, electronic, mechanical, photocopying, recording, or otherwise, without the prior written permission of the copyright holder.

Manufactured in the United States of America

CONTENTS

INTRODUCTION

Primary sources are the best way to get close to people from the past. They include the things people wrote in diaries, letters, or books; the paintings, drawings, maps, or cartoons they created; and even the buildings they constructed, the clothes they wore, or the possessions they owned. Such sources often reveal a lot about how people saw themselves and how they thought about their world.

This book collects a range of primary sources from the colonial period, from Christopher Columbus's arrival in Hispaniola in 1492 to the outbreak of the Revolutionary War in 1765. Over nearly 300 years European powers led by Spain, France, and England established settlements and political power in the Americas. Spain dominated South and Central America, and what is now the U.S. Southwest; the French were concentrated in what is now Canada.

The English took over much of the East Coast, establishing the Thirteen Colonies. As the numbers of settlers grew, including large numbers of slaves and indentured servants, so cities began to emege. Meanwhile, the impact on the native inhabitants of America increased as settlers encroached on their territory. Over generations, some Americans came to believe they had little connection with their rulers in Britain.

HOW TO USE THIS BOOK

Each spread contains at least one primary source. Look out for "Source Explored" boxes that explain images from the colonial period and who made them and why. There are also "As They Saw It" boxes that contain quotes from people of the period.

Some boxes contain more detailed information about a particular aspect of a subject. The subjects are arranged in roughly chronological order. They focus on key events or people. There is a full timeline of the period at the back of the book.

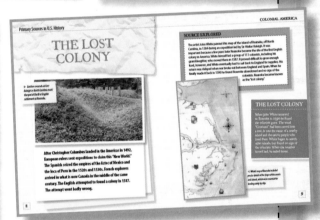

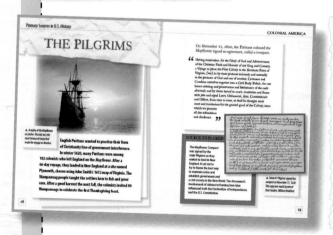

Some spreads feature a longer extract from a contemporary eyewitness. Look for the colored introduction that explains who the writer is and the origin of his or her account. These accounts are often accompanied by a related visual primary source.

NATIVE AMERICANS

When Europeans first arrived in America they did not find an empty continent. Up to ten million Native Americans lived in 600 tribes from the Pacific Northwest to the desert Southwest and the eastern woodlands. Within a century of Christopher Columbus's arrival in 1492, more than half the Native population had died. This was partly due to warfare, but mainly because of the introduction of European diseases, to which Native peoples had no resistance.

▲ Spaniards raise a cross (left) as Christopher Columbus (center) meets Native Americans in this engraving.

The manner of their attire and painting them selves when they goe to their generall huntings or at theire Solemne feasts.

◀ John White painted this Algonquin warrior in 1585 or 1586. Europeans were fascinated by the way Native Americans painted their bodies.

AS THEY SAW IT

" We are unarmed, and willing to give you what you ask, if you come in a friendly manner.... I am not so simple as not to know it is better to eat good meat, sleep comfortably, live quietly with my women and children, laugh and be merry with the English, and being their friend, trade for their copper and hatchets, than to run away from them.... "

—Powhatan, chief of the Algonquin Confederacy, addresses English settlers at Werowocomoco, Virginia, in 1609.

SOURCE EXPLORED

John White's watercolor *Indian in Body Paint* was painted in 1585 or 1586. White was the artist and mapmaker on an English expedition exploring North Carolina. His picture of an Algonquin elder was the first realistic image Europeans saw of a Native American. The man wears a deerskin loincloth and carries a quiver of arrows and a six-foot bow, so he may be dressed for war or a ritual. A puma tail hangs from his waist. His chest, calves, arms, and face are painted, and he has turkey feathers in his hair. His elaborate bracelets, earrings, and wrist guard are typical of the Southeastern Algonquin. The man's graying hair suggests he is an elder, and White painted him with tawny skin.

THE LOST COLONY

▶ *Earthen mounds at Fort Raleigh in North Carolina mark the spot of the first English settlement at Roanoke.*

After Christopher Columbus landed in 1492, European rulers sent expeditions to claim this "New World." The Spanish seized the empires of the Aztec of Mexico and the Inca of Peru in the 1520s and 1530s. French explorers arrived in what is now Canada in the middle of the same century. The English attempted to found a colony in 1587. The attempt went badly wrong.

SOURCE EXPLORED

The artist John White painted this map of the island of Roanoke, off North Carolina, in 1584 during an expedition led by Sir Walter Raleigh. It was important because a few years later Roanoke became the site of the first English colony in America. White himself led a group of 111 colonists, including his granddaughter, who moved there in 1587. It proved difficult to grow enough food, however, and White eventually had to sail back to England for supplies. His return was delayed when war broke out between England and Spain. When he finally made it back in 1590 he found Roanoke abandoned and no sign of the colonists. Roanoke became known as the "lost colony."

THE LOST COLONY

When John White returned to Roanoke in 1590 he found the colonists gone. The word "Croatoan" had been carved into a tree. It was the name of a nearby island and the Native people who lived there. White began to search other islands, but found no sign of the colonists. When the weather turned bad, he sailed home.

◄ White's map of Roanoke included precise details of the shape of the coasts and islands, which were essential for landing safely by ship.

SPANISH AMERICA

▲ *This church in Isleta Pueblo in New Mexico was built by Spanish priests, but in the local style of architecture.*

After Columbus' first voyage, the Spanish king and queen were eager to fund further exploration in America. The Spanish established colonies on Caribbean islands. From Hispaniola and Cuba they began to explore the American mainland. Hernán Cortés conquered the Aztec of Mexico in 1521 and Francisco Pizarro conquered the Inca of Peru in 1533. Spain grew fabulously rich from the gold and silver mines of its American empire—and more and more Spaniards were attracted to try and make their fortunes there.

Christopher Columbus explains to the Spanish monarchs, Ferdinand and Isabella, why he gave gifts to native peoples in return for supplies during his first voyage in 1492.

" I did this in order that I might more easily conciliate [please] them, that they might be led to become Christians, and be inclined to entertain a regard for the King and Queen, our Princes and all Spaniards, and that I might induce them to take an interest in seeking out, and collecting, and delivering to us things as they possessed in abundance, but which we greatly needed. **"**

▲ *This engraving was made in Spain in 1646. It shows the Virgin Mary watching over a Spanish ship near Chile.*

SOURCE EXPLORED

This Spanish engraving shows the Virgin Mary holding an anchor chain to save a Spanish galleon [ship] during a storm near a Spanish city in Chile. The print suggests that the Spanish empire enjoyed heavenly blessing. Many people saw creating an empire was a Christian duty, because it helped spread the Catholic faith. Many priests traveled to America to convert native peoples.

FRENCH AMERICA

As Spain grew wealthy thanks to its American colonies, the French monarchs staked their own claim to the New World. They tried to establish a colony in Florida in the 1560s but were driven off by the Spanish. Instead, the French turned their attention to the far north in the hope of finding a Northwest Passage to Asia and its valuable Spice Islands. They failed to find such a route, but French explorers found a vast land with ample wood, fish, and animal furs. This land was Canada.

▼ European demand for animal furs—especially beaver—would make Canada a wealthy colony.

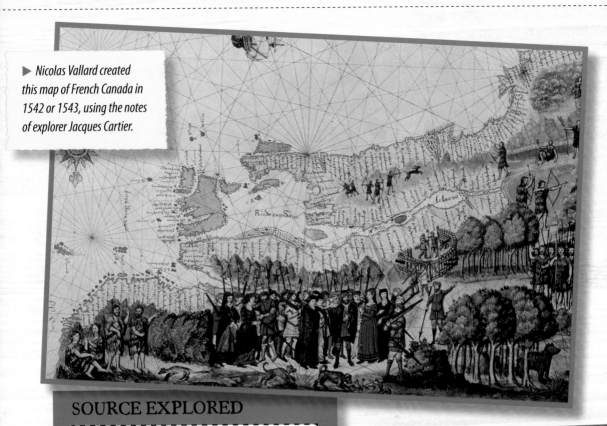

▶ Nicolas Vallard created this map of French Canada in 1542 or 1543, using the notes of explorer Jacques Cartier.

SOURCE EXPLORED

The Vallard Map is a record of early French exploration of Canada. It shows the St. Lawrence Valley, along with a group of French colonists led by Jean-François de La Rocque de Roberval. It also shows local Iroquois and a bear in the woods. The map contains the first use of the word "Kanata"—"Canada"—a Native word for a village that explorers mistakenly used as the name of the whole region. The map was based on the notes of Jacques Cartier, who in 1543 explored Prince Edward Island and the Gulf of St. Lawrence when the French king sent him to try to discover the Northwest Passage.

AS THEY SAW IT

66 Sieur de Champlain began to speak, and told [the Hurons] that he had always loved them, that he wished very much to have them as his brothers... and that the Iroquois had treacherously killed two or three of our men... and that the French cherished their friends very dearly... 99

—Paul le Jeune recalls Samuel de Champlain, governor of New France, making an alliance with the Hurons.

THE ENGLISH IN VIRGINIA

▲ This tower is all that remains of the church built by English settlers at Jamestown, Virginia, in 1639.

After the failed colony at Roanoke, it was not until 1607 that another English colony was established in Virginia, named for the English queen Elizabeth I, known as the "Virgin Queen." In 1607 the Virginia Company of London set up a colony at Jamestown. The first years of settlement were very difficult, however. In what became known as the Starving Time, only 150 of 500 settlers survived the winter of 1609–1610. One of the leaders of the new colony was John Smith, who recorded its early days.

In *The Generall Historie of Virginia* (1624) Captain John Smith described building Jamestown and exploring Virginia.

" Now fell every man to work. The Council contrive [plan and build] the Fort, the rest cut down trees to make place to pitch their tents; some provide clapboard to relade [reload] the ships, some make gardens, some nets, etc. The savages often visited us kindly...

Newport, Smith and twenty others, were sent to discover the head of the river; by divers small habitants they passed, in six days they arrived at a town called Powhatan, consisting of some twelve houses, pleasantly seated on a hill... of this place the Prince is called Powhatan, and his people Powhatans. **"**

SOURCE EXPLORED

John Smith traveled up to 2,500 miles in a series of short expeditions across the Chesapeake region of Virginia to produce this first-ever detailed map of Virginia in 1612. Smith's map was so accurate it stayed in use for the next seven years. The map shows more than 200 Native towns as well as rivers, tributaries, bays, islands, and the shoreline. Smith used cross symbols to mark the boundaries of the areas he had actually seen for himself.

◀ *John Smith produced his 1612 map of Virginia partly in order to encourage English settlers to move to North America.*

POCAHONTAS

The English settlers at Jamestown only survived because they were helped by the local chief, Powhatan, who ruled about 8,500 people. Powhatan gave the English food and showed them how to grow crops such as corn. Powhatan's daughter, known as Pocahontas, taught John Smith the Powhatan language and acted as a go-between between the colonists and her father.

She had saved Smith's life after Powhatan threatened to kill him. Pocahontas went on to marry an Englishman, John Rolfe, and convert to Christianity. She sailed to London, where she met the royal family. She died of smallpox on her way back to America.

◀ *This drawing by Smith shows Powhatan wearing a headdress as the Powhatan meet to decide Smith's fate.*

SOURCE EXPLORED

In this 1632 image by John Smith, Pocahontas wears the clothes of an elegant Englishwoman. The portrait, which appeared in Smith's *The Generall Historie of Virginia*, reflects the dramatic change in Pocahontas' life after her marriage to the English plantation owner John Rolfe. At the edge of the portrait Smith noted her other names: Matoaka and Rebecca, the name she took after she became a Christian.

▲ *The large lace ruff that Pocahontas wears in this portrait was the height of European fashion in the 1630s.*

John Smith remembers how he was threatened with death after being captured by the Powhatans while hunting for food.

❝ At [Smith's] entrance before the king, all the people gave a great shout. The queen of Appamatuck was appointed to bring him [Smith] water to wash his hands, and another brought him a bunch of feathers, instead of a towel to dry them. Having feasted him after their best barbarous manner they could, a long consultation was held but the conclusion was, two great stones were brought before Powhatan: then as many as could laid hands on him, dragged him to them, and thereon laid his head, and being ready with their clubs to beat out his brains, Pocahontas, the king's dearest daughter, when no entreaty [pleading] could prevail, got his head in her arms, and laid her own upon his to save him from death: whereat the emperor was contented he should live... ❞

THE PILGRIMS

▲ *A replica of the Mayflower at anchor. The ship was the most famous of many that made the voyage to America.*

English Puritans wanted to practice their form of Christianity free of government interference. In winter 1620, many Puritans were among 102 colonists who left England on the *Mayflower*. After a sixty-six-day voyage, they landed in New England at a site named Plymouth, chosen using John Smith's 1612 map of Virginia. The Wampanoag people taught the settlers how to fish and grow corn. After a good harvest the next fall, the colonists invited ninety Wampanoags to celebrate the first Thanksgiving feast.

On November 11, 1620, the Puritans onboard the *Mayflower* signed an agreement, called a compact.

> " Having undertaken, for the Glory of God and Advancement of the Christian Faith and Honour of our King and Country, a Voyage to plant the First Colony in the Northern Parts of Virginia, [we] do by these presents solemnly and mutually in the presence of God and one of another, Covenant and Combine ourselves together into a Civil Body Politic, for our better ordering and preservation and furtherance of the ends aforesaid; and by virtue hereof to enact, constitute and frame such just and equal Laws, Ordinances, Acts, Constitutions and Offices, from time to time, as shall be thought most meet and convenient for the general good of the Colony, unto which we promise all due submission and obedience. "

SOURCE EXPLORED

The Mayflower Compact was signed by the male Pilgrims as they waited to land in New England. It set out to try to frame the best way to maintain order and establish government and a civil society in the New World. The document's involvement of citizens in framing laws later influenced both the Declaration of Independence and the U.S. Constitution.

▲ *Some 41 Pilgrims signed the compact on November 11, 1620. This copy was made by one of their leaders, William Bradford.*

SALEM WITCH TRIALS

In the "Great Migration" of 1630 more than a thousand Puritans reached America in eleven ships. On June 12, 1630, they founded the town of Salem, Massachusetts. Late in the century, the town's strict laws and the Puritan belief in witchcraft caused a notorious series of trials. In 1692 and 1693, young girls began to accuse many local people of being witches or being possessed by Satan. Twenty people, mostly women, were put to death.

▼ This memorial to one of the executed women is part of a memorial opened in Salem in 1992, 300 years after the trials.

BRIDGET BISHOP
HANGED
JUNE 10, 1692

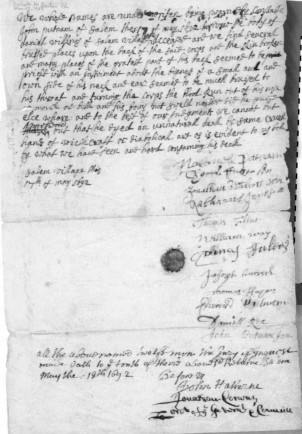

SOURCE EXPLORED

Daniel Wilkins lived in Salem. After he died in May 1692, the local constable, John Putnam, and other witnesses examined his body. They decided that his injuries were unusual and a sign that he had been a victim of witchcraft. In this document, they list the injuries they think prove the evidence of witchcraft. They include the fact that Wilkins' neck and ear were bruised near his throat and that his corpse bled from its nose and mouth.

◀ After Wilkins' death was ruled to be caused by witchcraft, a local man was tried and executed for causing it.

Samuel Sewall, a Boston businessman and judge, served as a magistrate at the trials and recorded them in his diary.

" April 11, 1692. Went to Salem, where, in the meeting-house, the persons accused of witchcraft were examined; was a very great assembly; 'twas awful to see how the afflicted persons were agitated. Mr. Noyes pray'd at the beginning, and Mr. Higginson concluded.

Monday, September 19, 1692. About noon, at Salem, Giles corey was press'd to death for standing mute [not talking under torture]; much pains was used with him two days, one after another, by the Court and Capt. Gardner of Nantucket: but all in vain. "

PENNSYLVANIA AND THE QUAKERS

▲ *This German print from the 1770s shows Philadelphia as a thriving port that resembles a city in Europe.*

In 1681, King Charles II granted William Penn a huge area of North America to form a new colony. Penn, a devout Quaker, founded Pennsylvania for his fellow Quakers. Their refusal to acknowledge the superiority of kings made them unpopular in Europe. In many ways Pennsylvania was a model colony: settlers and Native Americans lived in relative harmony. Penn established the city of Philadelphia. By 1700, 10,000 people lived in the thriving city.

William Penn wrote The Propriety of Pennsylvania in 1682 in order to encourage settlers from Europe to come to his new colony. The document makes clear his admiration for the Native Americans and describes how he bought land from them.

" When the purchase was agreed, great promises passed between us of kindness and good neighbourhood, and that the Indians and English must live in love, as long as the sun gave light. Which done, another made a speech to the Indians, in the name of all the Sachamakers or kings, first to tell them what was done; next, to charge and command them, to love the Christians, and particularly to live in peace with me, and the people under my government... "

SOURCE EXPLORED

This engraving was made in 1775 and based on contemporary images and accounts. It shows Penn, in black clothes and hat, negotiating with the Lenape (also known as the Delaware). The Lenape are examining goods Penn is offering them. Penn insisted on buying land, rather than simply taking it.

◄ The scene of Penn's land deal was painted by the artist Benjamin West and engraved by John Hall in 1775.

NEW NETHERLAND

In 1624 Dutch settlers established New Netherland, around what is now New York City. They traded with native peoples for fur. The Dutch colony lay between the English colonies of Massachusetts and Virginia, and in 1664 King Charles II of England sent warships to take it over. The unpopular Dutch governor, Peter Stuyvesant, tried to resist but had no support. The New Netherlands became English territory and was renamed New York.

▼ *Johannes Vingboons painted this view of the southern tip of Manhattan in 1664, the year the English captured New Amsterdam and renamed it New York.*

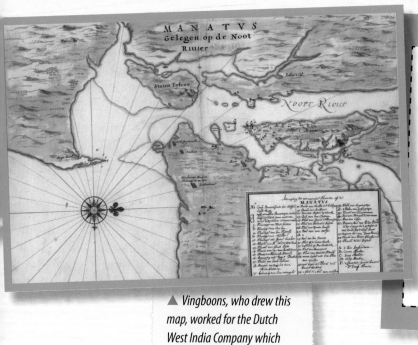

This map of New York Harbor was painted in 1639, probably by the Dutch artist Johannes Vingboons. It shows "Manatus," or Manhattan (center, right), and the North River, the Dutch name for the Hudson River. It depicts Dutch farms, with a key listing their owners. Native American settlements are shown by longhouses. (North is to the right).

▲ Vingboons, who drew this map, worked for the Dutch West India Company which governed New Netherland.

Junker Van Der Donck was a member of a committee that reported on conditions in New Netherland for the Dutch West Indian Company. He predicted that Governor Peter Stuyvesant's poor running of the colony would lead to its loss.

" Stuyvesant's first arrival—for what passed on the voyage is not for us to speak of—was like a peacock, with great state and pomp. The appellation of Lord General, and similar titles, were never before known here. Almost every day he caused proclamations of various import [importance] to be published, which were for the most part never observed, and have long since been a dead letter, except the Fine excise [taxation], as that yielded a profit...

In our opinion this country will never flourish under the government of the Honorable Company, but will pass away and come to an end of itself, unless the Honorable Company be reformed. "

TOWNS AND CITIES

▼ *This early drawing shows the growing skyline of Philadelphia, with church towers and large houses.*

During the seventeenth century, English settlements began to grow. In New England, the Massachusetts Bay Company ruled that towns should have a meeting house, which was also a town hall and a church, and common land available for all citizens. From 1647, towns with more than fifty people had to hire a teacher. Meanwhile, harbor settlements such as Boston and New York grew into large cities. By 1750, Boston had 20,000 inhabitants, and New York was even larger.

Benjamin Franklin was brought up in Boston but after a fight with his brother moved to Philadelphia in 1723, aged 17.

" [I] arrived there [in Philadelphia] about 8 or 9 o'clock, in the Sunday morning and landed at the Market Street wharf...
Then I walked up the street, gazing about, till near the Market House I met a boy with bread. I had made many a meal on bread, and inquiring where he got it, I went immediately to the baker's he directed me to in Second Street; and asked for a biscuit, intending such as we had in Boston, but they it seems were not made in Philadelphia... I walked again up the street, which by this time had many clean dressed people in it who were all walking the same way. I joined them, and thereby was led into the great Meeting House of the Quakers near the Market... "

SOURCE EXPLORED

The Castello Plan shows Lower Manhattan around 1660. The shape of the city is already becoming clear. After the English took over, New York grew rapidly. It went from having about 1,500 people in the 1660s to just under 20,000 around 1700 and 117,000 in 1760.

▼ The Castello Plan is named for the Italian villa where it was found in 1900. It was drawn by Jacques Cortelyou in 1660.

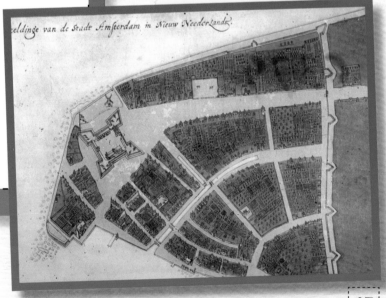

NEW ARRIVALS

The British colonies in North America attracted a variety of settlers. Some were seeking religious freedom. Others came to try to make their fortunes, perhaps by growing tobacco in Virginia. For many, the colonies were an opportunity to improve their lot. Even very poor Europeans could become "indentured servants." Their passage to America was paid in return for up to seven years of labor, often at hard tasks later done by black slaves.

▼ This 1761 engraving shows Bethlehem, Pennsylvania, founded by German Moravaians who wanted freedom to practice their religion.

NOVA BRITANNIA.

OFFRING MOST

Excellent fruites by Planting in
VIRGINIA.

Exciting all such as be well affected
to further the same.

C. 2263.

LONDON.
Printed for SAMVEL MACHAM, and are to be sold at
his Shop in Pauls Church-yard, at the
Signe of the Bul-head.
1 6 0 9.

AS THEY SAW IT

"" Warm food is served only
three times a week, the
rations being very poor and
very little. Such meals can
hardly be eaten, on account
of being so unclean. The
water which is served out of
the ships is often very black,
thick, and full of worms, so
that one cannot drink it. ""

—Gottlieb Mittelburger describes
crossing the Atlantic in **1750**.

◀ *The booklet published by
Robert Johnson in 1609 was
only the third publication to
be written about Virginia.*

SOURCE EXPLORED

This illustration comes from a booklet published in 1609. It was one of the
first publications to encourage colonists to move to Virginia. Its author,
Robert Johnson, was a member of the Virginia Company that organized
English settlement, or "planting," in North America. The book offers "excellent
fruites," meaning opportunities to make money. A few years later the colonist
John Rolfe, husband of Pocahontas, imported tobacco to Virginia from
Bermuda. It grew well in the Virginia soil and climate, and tobacco became
the leading crop. It was exported in huge quantities to Europe, where smoking
had become highly fashionable. By 1670 half of all English adult men smoked
tobacco every day—and virtually all of it came from Virginia.

TRADE

Colonial America was built on trade. The earliest colonists traded with Native Americans and later colonists bartered for goods, swapping surplus crops for what they needed. As the American economy grew, the colonies raised huge revenues for Britain through duties that had to be paid on all imports to or exports from the colonies. Ships sailed across the Atlantic loaded with European luxuries such as tea and coffee. They returned to England with American tobacco and timber.

▼ *One of the largest American exports to Britain was timber, which was particularly important for building ships.*

Pehr [Peter] Kalm was a Swedish plant collector. From 1748 he spent two years in Pennsylvania, New Jersey, and New York.

" New York probably carries on a more extensive commerce than any town in the English North American provinces; at least it may be said to equal them: Boston and Philadelphia however come very near to it. The trade of New York extends to many places; and it is said they send more ships from thence to London, than they do from Philadelphia. They export to that capital all the various sorts of skins which they buy of the Indians, sugar, logwood, and other dying woods, rum, mahogany, and many other goods which are the produce of the West Indies; together with all the specie [money] which they get in the course of trade. **"**

SOURCE EXPLORED

This eighteenth-century woodcut was used in England to label tobacco from Virginia. It shows two crudely drawn Native Americans smoking clay pipes and drinking from a large vat. Many similar labels also featured Native Americans. For storekeepers in England, the association with Native culture was positive. It suggested that the tobacco was authentic.

◀ Tobacco labels in the eighteenth and early nineteenth centuries often featured Native Americans or African slaves.

TRANSPORTATION

▲ The Conestoga wagon was used from the late eighteenth century. It was sturdy and high above the ground, so it could cope with rough terrain.

The colonies covered a huge area, so it was difficult to move around. Rivers were important highways. Like the Native Americans, some colonists used canoes to get around. Most roads were just muddy tracks, so people used horses to travel. By 1680, 80 percent of farmers in Chesapeake owned at least one horse. But there were no road signs and few bridges, and travel at night was dangerous because it was often too dark to see anything.

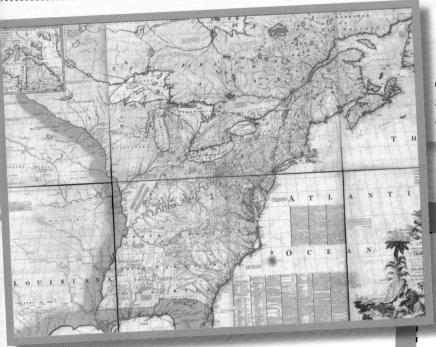

◀ In 1775 John Mitchell drew a map of the British colonies showing roads and the distance between settlements.

SOURCE EXPLORED

This map of the British colonies was drawn for the British government. Political unrest was gathering. It would eventually lead to the Revolutionary War. The map showed all the roads in the region. Such a map would prove very useful to British military commanders if the expected war began.

Sarah Kemble Knight was a businesswoman who kept a diary of a journey she made through New England in 1704.

" Wednesday, October 4th, 1704.
About four in the morning, we set out... This Rode was poorly furnished with accommodations for Travellers... which I exceedingly complained of....

Friday, October 6th, 1704.
We advanced on towards Seabrook. The Rodes all along this way are very bad, Incumbred with Rocks and mountainous passages, which were very disagreeable to my tired carcass; but we went on with a moderate pace which made ye Journy more pleasant. But after about eight miles Rideing, in going over a Bridge under which the River Run very swift, my hors stumbled, and very narrowly 'scaped [escaped] falling into the water... "

RELIGION

▲ Mennonites—Protestants from Germany—built this meeting house in Germantown, Philadelphia, in 1770.

Religious tolerance was an early attraction of North America for European colonists. Some practiced variations of Protestant Christianity, such as the Puritans and the Moravians; others were Quakers; communities of Jews also arrived. Within the colonies a lack of established churches encouraged more evangelical forms of religion, in which a formal structure of priests and bishops was not important.

◀ George Whitefield was a leader of the "Great Awakening" of the 1740s. More Great Awakenings followed later in the eighteenth century.

AS THEY SAW IT

" I hardly ever knew him go through a sermon without weeping... Sometimes he exceedingly wept, stamped loudly and passionately, and was frequently so overcome, that, for a few seconds, you would suspect he never could recover; and when he did, nature required some little time to compose himself. "

—Cornelius Winter, Whitefield's assistant

SOURCE EXPLORED

This portrait was engraved by Elisha Gallaudet in New York in 1774. It was used to illustrate the memoirs of the man it shows, George Whitefield. Whitefield was a famous preacher, and the portrait shows him in the middle of delivering a sermon with his hands raised toward heaven. Whitefield was a small cross-eyed man, but he electrified congregations. It was claimed that his voice could be heard two miles away. Whitefield was an Englishman who moved to Savannah, Georgia, in 1738 to serve as a parish priest. He began preaching throughout the colonies and in the early 1740s was a leader of a movement known as the "First Great Awakening," a great surge in the popularity of evangelical Protestantism in America. He became one of the first celebrities in the colonies, and in 1742 preached to a crowd of around 30,000 people.

CULTURAL LIFE

As the colonies grew more established, colonists started to have more free time. The things they liked to do were the same as they had enjoyed in the Old World. In cities, people went to the theater, listened to or played music, and enjoyed art. In the country, outdoor activities included ice skating and sledding in winter and cock-fighting and bull-baiting in the summer. At home, people read newspapers and books as literacy levels grew and printing made publications cheaper.

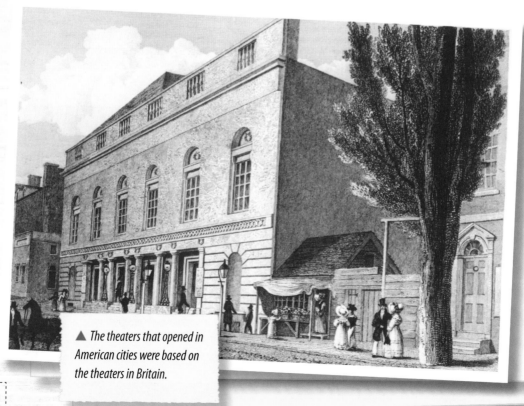

▲ The theaters that opened in American cities were based on the theaters in Britain.

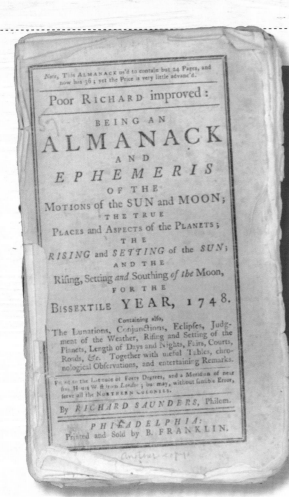

Note, This ALMANACK us'd to contain but 24 Pages, and now has 36; yet the Price is very little advanc'd.

Poor RICHARD improved:

BEING AN

ALMANACK

AND

EPHEMERIS

OF THE

MOTIONS of the SUN and MOON;

THE TRUE

PLACES and ASPECTS of the PLANETS;

THE

RISING and *SETTING* of the *SUN;*

AND THE

Rising, Setting *and* Southing *of the* Moon,

FOR THE

BISSEXTILE YEAR, 1748.

Containing also,

The Lunations, Conjunctions, Eclipses, Judgment of the Weather, Rising and Setting of the Planets, Length of Days and Nights, Fairs, Courts, Roads, &c. Together with useful Tables, chronological Observations, and entertaining Remarks.

Fitted to the Latitude of Forty Degrees, and a Meridian of near five Hours West from London; but may, without sensible Error, serve all the NORTHERN COLONIES.

By *RICHARD SAUNDERS*, Philom.

PHILADELPHIA:

Printed and Sold by B. FRANKLIN.

SOURCE EXPLORED

This is the title page from *Poor Richard's Almanack* for 1748. Poor Richard was a pen name for Benjamin Franklin, who published the almanac every year from 1732 to 1758. Almanacs gave information like the times of sunrise and sunset on each day to help people follow the calendar. Franklin included entertaining sayings, which made the book very popular. It sold up to 10,000 copies.

◀ *The title page of* Poor Richard's Almanack *for 1748 lists Franklin's name at the very bottom.*

As a young man, the Founding Father and scientist Benjamin Franklin learned to be a printer by working on *The New England Courant,* founded by his brother in 1721. Of it he wrote:

❝ The only one before it was *The Boston News Letter*. I remember his being dissuaded by some friends from the undertaking, as not likely to succeed, one newspaper being in their judgment enough for America... He went on, however, with the undertaking, and after having worked in composing the types and printing off the sheets I was employed to carry the papers thro' the streets to meet customers. He had some ingenious men among his friends who amused themselves by writing little pieces for this paper, which gained it credit, and made it more in demand. ❞

SLAVERY

▲ *On colonial plantations, slaves lived together in small, simple quarters like these slave huts in South Carolina.*

From the arrival of the first African slaves in Virginia in 1619, the slave trade grew rapidly. From the 1670s, slaves were used mainly in southern colonies, where tobacco and cotton were grown on large estates. By 1700, 43 percent of South Carolina's population was made up of African slaves. Gradually a gap opened between the attitudes toward slavery in the South and in the North, where many Americans believed it was immoral.

SOURCE EXPLORED

This plan shows how slaves were to be stowed beneath decks on the British slave ship *Brookes*. The slaves were shackled with iron chains so that they could not move. This plan was drawn up in 1788, after an act of Parliament had limited the number of slaves British ships could carry. Throughout the Colonial period there had been no limits, and conditions were far more crowded. Slaves were crammed so close together that some died during the crossing. If they were allowed on deck for fresh air and exercise, some jumped overboard to escape, even though they knew they would drown. Even after the Regulated Slave Trade Act, the passage to North America was highly traumatic for the slaves.

AS THEY SAW IT

" One day, when all our people were gone out to their works as usual, and only I and my dear sister were left to mind the house, two men and a woman got over our walls, and in a moment seized us both; and, without giving us time to cry out, or to make resistance, they stopped our mouths, tied our hands, and ran off with us into the nearest wood. "

—Olaudah Equiano describes being kidnapped from his African village by African slave traders at the age of 11.

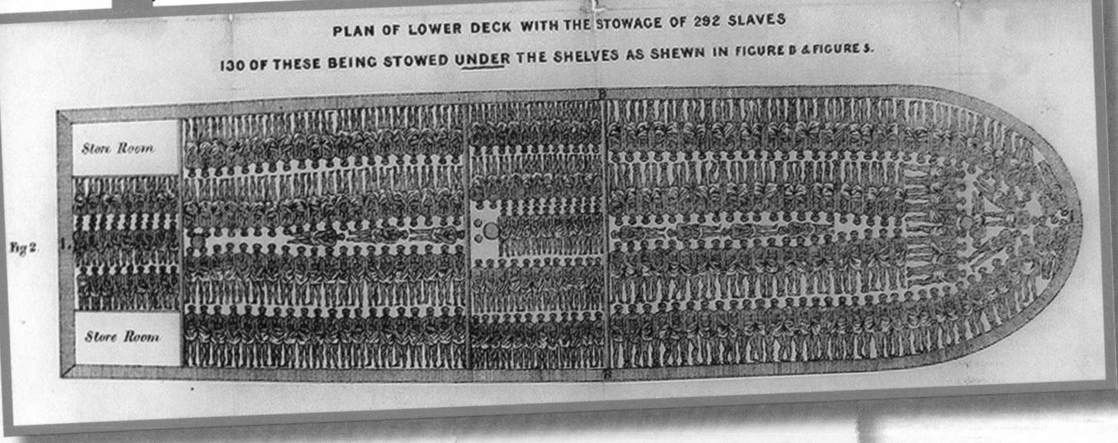

PLAN OF LOWER DECK WITH THE STOWAGE OF 292 SLAVES
130 OF THESE BEING STOWED UNDER THE SHELVES AS SHEWN IN FIGURE B & FIGURE 5.

Store Room

Fig 2.

Store Room

▲ During the voyage from Africa, slaves were chained up on decks that were so low it was barely possible for them to stand up without banging their heads.

FRENCH AND INDIAN WAR

In 1756 the Seven Years' War began in Europe. Britain and its allies fought the French and their allies. The conflict spread to North America, where it is called the French and Indian War, because the French fought with their Iroquois allies. The French won a series of battles but eventually British troops were victorious. At the end of the war, the defeated French handed Canada to the British.

▼ *The British general James Wolfe lies dying after the attack on Quebec in September 1759 that turned the war in Britain's favor.*

JOIN, or DIE.

SOURCE EXPLORED

This cartoon appeared in the *Pennsylvania Gazette* on May 9, 1754. Its creator, Benjamin Franklin, shows the colonies as a snake. Franklin meant that the colonies should work together with Britain in the coming war. In the American Revolution, the cartoon became a symbol of unity against the British.

In March 1758 thirteen-year-old Mary Jeminson and her family were captured by Iroquois who raided their frontier village.

“ The party that took us consisted of six Indians and four Frenchmen... They set out with their prisoners in great haste, for fear of detection, and soon entered the woods. On our march that day, an Indian went behind us with a whip, with which he frequently lashed the children, to make them keep up. In this manner we traveled till dark, without a mouthful of food or a drop of water, although we had not eaten since the night before... At night they encamped in the woods, without fire and without shelter, where we were watched with the greatest vigilance. Extremely fatigued, and very hungry, we were compelled to lie upon the ground, without supper or a drop of water. ”

PROCLAMATION OF 1763

▲ Colonial Americans were eager to cross the Appalachians and settle in the Ohio Valley, but were forbidden to do so.

The expansion of British territory alarmed Native Americans, who were losing their land. To reassure them, King George III (reigned 1760–1820) issued a proclamation that recognized the right of Native Americans to own land and set out the limits of the British colonies. The colonists resented this intervention in the right to expand west.

SOURCE EXPLORED

This copy of the Royal Proclamation of 1763 was issued by John Penn, who was the British lieutenant governor of Pennsylvania. Penn was King George III's representative in the colony, and was responsible for enacting British laws there. Penn had the king's proclamation printed so that its contents could be widely distributed and displayed. The document has a prominent crest at the top, to show that it is an official document. The printer's name is also included at the bottom, which is more evidence that the document is authentic. It finishes with the motto "God Save the King!" which is a reminder that Penn was acting on behalf of George III.

BY THE HONOURABLE

JOHN PENN, Esq;

Lieutenant-Governor and Commander in Chief of the Province of *Pennsylvania*, and Counties of *New-Castle, Kent* and *Suffex*, on *Delaware*,

A PROCLAMATION.

WHEREAS I have received Information, That on *Wednesday*, the Fourteenth Day of this Month, a Number of People, armed, and mounted on Horseback, unlawfully assembled together, and went to the *Indian* Town in the *Coneftogoe* Manor, in *Lancaster* County, and without the least Reason or Provocation, in cool Blood, barbarously killed six of the *Indians* settled there, and burnt and destroyed all their Houses and Effects: AND WHEREAS so cruel and in-human an Act, committed in the Heart of this Province on the said *Indians*, who have lived peaceably and inoffensively among us, during all our late Troubles, and for many Years before, and were justly considered as under the Protection of this Government and its Laws, calls loudly for the vigorous Exertion of the civil Authority, to detect the Offenders, and bring them to condign Punishment: I HAVE THEREFORE, by and with the Advice and Consent of the Council, thought fit to issue this Proclamation, and do hereby strictly charge and enjoin all Judges, Justices, Sheriffs, Constables, Officers Civil and Military, and all other His Majesty's liege Subjects within this Province, to make diligent Search and Enquiry after the Authors and Perpetrators of the said Crime, their Abettors and Accomplices, and to use all possible Means to apprehend and secure them in some of the public Goals of this Province, that they may be brought to their Trials, and be proceeded against according to Law.

AND WHEREAS a Number of other *Indians*, who lately lived on or near the Frontiers of this Province, being willing and desirous to preserve and continue the ancient Friendship which here-tofore subsisted between them and the good People of this Province, have, at their own earnest Re-quest, been removed from their Habitations, and brought into the County of *Philadelphia*, and seat-ed, for the present, for their better Security, on the *Province-Island*, and in other Places in the Neighbourhood of the City of *Philadelphia*, where Provision is made for them at the public Expence. I do therefore hereby strictly forbid all Persons whatsoever, to molest or injure any of the said *Indians*, as they will answer the contrary at their Peril.

GIVEN *under my Hand and the Great Seal of the said Province, at Philadelphia, the Twenty-second Day of December, Anno Domini One Thousand Seven Hundred and Sixty-three, and in the Fourth Year of His Majesty's Reign.*

JOHN PENN.

By His Honour's Command,
JOSEPH SHIPPEN, *junior, Secretary.*

GOD Save the KING.

PHILADELPHIA: Printed by B. FRANKLIN, and D. HALL.

▲ *The proclamation was printed so that it could be passed around or placed on walls for everyone to read.*

AS THEY SAW IT

❝ [So] that the Indians may be convinced of our Justice and determined Resolution to remove all reasonable Cause of Discontent, We do... strictly enjoin and require that no private Person do presume to make any purchase from the said Indians of any Lands reserved to the said Indians, within those parts of our Colonies where we have thought proper to allow Settlement. ❞

—Extract from the Proclamation of 1763

TIMELINE

1492	Christopher Columbus lands in Hispaniola.
1524	Giovanni d Verrazano explores the North American coast and discovers New York Bay.
1521	The Spanish overthrow the Aztec in Mexico.
1533	The Spanish overthrow the Inca in Peru.
1534	Jacques Cartier explores the St. Lawrence River for Canada
1565	The Spanish found St. Augustine in Florida.
1584	Sir Walter Raleigh claims Virginia in the name of Queen Elizabeth I of England.
1587	The English found a settlement at Roanoke; three years later the colony is mysteriously abandoned.
1607	Captain John Smith and settlers build a settlement on the James River in Virginia.
1608	Samuel de Champlain establishes a trading fort in Canda that will become Quebec.
1612	Colonists in Virginia begin to grow tobacco.
1619	The first ship carrying African slaves arrives in Virginia.
1624	The Dutch "buy" Manhattan Island from native peoples.
1643	New Sweden is established on the Delaware River.
1664	The English annex New Netherland and rename it New York.
1673	The Boston Post Road is built.
1675	In King Philip's War, Metacomet (King Philip) attacks English settlers.
1688	In King William's War, Alonguin tribes ally with the French to fight the English and their Iroquois allies.
1692	In Salem, Massachusetts, courts convict and execute nineteen people for witchcraft.
1702	The English and French, with their Native allies, begin eleven years of fighting in Queen Anne's War.
1702	The French settle in Alabama.

1704	The Boston News-Letter *becomes the first regular newspaper in North America.*
1710	*English forces seize Acadia in Canada from the French.*
1713	*In the Treaty of Utrecht, France gives up colonial territory to England.*
1716	*The first theater in the colonies opens in Williamsburg, Virginia.*
1732	*James Oglethorpe founds Georgia, south of Carolina.*
1730s	*The Great Awakening sweeps through the British colonies.*
1730s	*Moravians establish settlements in Pennsylvania and, later, North Carolina.*
1738	*Indigo becomes a useful crop in South Carolina.*
1752	*Benjamin Franklin invents the lightning conductor.*
1754	*The French and Indian War begins.*
1759	*The British capture Quebec from the French.*
1763	*Chief Pontiac leads a Native rebellion against the British around Detroit.*
1760s	*Rice is grown in the lower colonies.*
1763	*The Treaty of Paris cedes Canada and the eastern United States to Britain.*
1763	*King George III issues the Proclamation of 1763, limiting British settlement west of the Appalachian Mountains.*

GLOSSARY

almanac An annual calendar that lists important dates and statistical information such as astronomical data and tide tables.

colony A settlement that is under the control of the govenrment of another country and that is populated by people from that country.

compact An agreement made by a number of people.

engraving A picture made by drawing an image on a sheet of metal and using it to print on paper.

evangelical A Christian or group of Christians that lives by the word of the Bible and tries to spread the faith.

galleon A large Spanish sailing ship used from the fifteenth to the eighteenth centuries.

indentured servant A servant who agrees to provide labor in order to repay a debt.

indigenous Describes the native people, animals, or plants of a particular region.

longhouse A traditional dwelling used by the Iroquois and other Native Americans.

meeting house A Quaker or Protestant place of worship and government.

Old World A phrase that refers to Europe, as opposed to the "New World," or America.

pen name A name used by an author that is not his or her real name.

plantation A large farm growing labor-intensive crops such as tobacco and sugar.

proclamation An official announcement that deals with a matter of great importance.

Puritan A person who follows a strict form of the Protestant religion.

revenue Income raised by a government from taxes and other fees.

FURTHER INFORMATION

Books

Hollar, Sherman. *Biographies of Colonial America*. Impact on America: Collective Biographies. New York, NY: Rosen Education Service, 2012.

McNeese, Tim. *Colonial America: 1543–1763*. Discovering U.S. History. New York, NY: Chelsea House Publishing, 2010.

Pratt, Mary K. *A Timeline History of the Thirteen Colonies*. Timeline Trackers: America's Beginnings. Minneapolis, MN: Lerner Publications, 2014.

Samuels, Charlie. *Timeline of the Colonial World*. History Highlights. New York, NY: Gareth Stevens, 2010.

Stanley, George E. *The European Settlement of North America 1492–1763*. Primary Source History of the United States. World Almanac Library, 2005.

Thompson, Linda. *America's First Settlements*. History of America. Vero Beach, FL: Rourke Educational Media, 2013.

Websites

www.americaslibrary.gov/jb/colonial/jb_colonial_subj.html
America's Library page on colonial America, with many links to stories.

www.history.com/topics/thirteen-colonies
History.com page with many videos about colonial America.

www.digitalhistory.uh.edu
Click on "Colonial Era" to access Digital History's resources for the period.

www.historyplace.com/unitedstates/revolution/rev-early.htm
Colonial America timeline on The History Place website.

Publisher's note to educators and parents: Our editors have carefully reviewed these websites to ensure that they are suitable for students. Many websites change frequently, however, and we cannot guarantee that a site's future contents will continue to meet our high standards of quality and educational value. Be advised that students should be closely supervised whenever they access the Internet.

INDEX